# BEATITUDES

This book belongs to

JANE     HYDE

©Disney

# A Worship Anthology on the
# BEATITUDES

## H. J. Richards

*Readings, Poems and Collects*

Kevin Mayhew

First published in 1995 by
KEVIN MAYHEW LTD
Rattlesden
Bury St Edmunds
Suffolk IP30 0SZ

ISBN 0 86209 714 2
Catalogue No 1500035

Front cover:
A stained glass window at Wissington Church, Suffolk
photographed by Alan Bedding

Cover design by Graham Johnstone and Veronica Ward
Typesetting and Page Creation by Louise Hill
Printed and bound in Great Britain.

# CONTENTS

# FOREWORD

The warm reception given to the two worship anthologies
I have recently published (one for Christmas and one for
Easter) has encouraged me to forage even further afield to
collect a greater variety of biblical texts, poems, readings,
meditations and prayers which could be used for worship
at other times of the year.

The anthology in this volume is based on the beatitudes or
blessings which Jesus pronounced on those who accepted
his teaching. Who are the lucky ones? Paradoxically he
congratulates the powerless nobodies of this world for their
good fortune, and challengingly repeats this eight times
over. These statements provide the chapter headings
which follow.


H. J. RICHARDS

# 1 THE BEATITUDES

## *Scripture Readings*

And seeing the multitudes,
he went up into a mountain,
and when he was set down,
his disciples came unto him.
And opening his mouth he taught them, saying:

Blessed are the poor in spirit:
    for theirs is the kingdom of heaven.
Blessed are the meek:
    for they shall possess the land.
Blessed are they that mourn:
    for they shall be comforted.
Blessed are they that hunger and thirst after justice:
    for they shall have their fill.
Blessed are the merciful:
    for they shall obtain mercy.
Blessed are the clean of heart:
    for they shall see God.
Blessed are the peacemakers:
    for they shall be called the children of God.
Blessed are they that suffer persecution for justice' sake:
    for theirs is the kingdom of heaven.

THE GOSPEL OF MATTHEW 5:1-10
(DOUAI VERSION)

How lucky you are if you are poor!
God will make you rich!

How lucky you are if you're not very important!
God will make you great!

How lucky you are if your heart has been broken!
It will mend even stronger!

How lucky you are if you're starving!
You'll get all you want, and more!

How lucky you are if you're tender with others!
You know how tender God really is!

How lucky you are if you're straight with people!
You see God very clearly indeed!

How lucky you are if you make friends with people!
You've brought a bit of heaven to earth!

How lucky you are if people hate you
    for standing up for what's right!
A new world can be built on people like you!


THE BEATITUDES FOR CHILDREN
H. J. RICHARDS (B. 1921)

You are blessed who are poor in desires,
never seeking the riches of earth, which the fires
can consume, turn to dust,
or the waters of fortune can rust;
the Kingdom is yours, you are just.

You are blessed who are sad, but whose crying
is not for yourself, for your self must be dying:
your tears shall have worth
when they share in the cares of the earth;
for a cross brings the Kingdom to birth.

You are blessed who are gentle and meek,
for the war-cries of rage are the tunes of the weak:
your silence is long,
and the trumpets of anger blow strong;
but the Kingdom will dance to your song.

You are blessed who make peace, who believe
not in weapons to conquer, to ravish, to grieve:
you find your employ
in creating what guns just destroy;
the name of God's sons you'll enjoy.

You are blessed when they seek you to kill,
and to wound like the master himself on a hill,
amid laughter and scorn;
so his wounds must be worn
to recall where the Kingdom was born.


MALCOLM STEWART (B. 1938)

Blest are you, O poor in spirit;
here is wealth beyond all telling.

Blest are you that faint with hunger;
here is food all want dispelling.

Blest are you that weep for sorrow;
endless gladness here is given.

Blest are you when men shall hate you;
I will be your joy in heaven.


JAMES QUINN

How blest you who are poor,
you who hold out your hands and beg day after day.
How blest you who are poor,
you who know that your bread comes only from God.
How blest you who are poor,
for the Kingdom of God is there in your hands.
    Alas for you who already have your fill,
    who put lock and key on the harvest in your barns;
    alas for you who don't know how to beg!

How blest all you who weep,
for a face bathed in tears is a face full of love.
How blest all you who weep,
and whose lives bear the mark of the sign of the Cross.
How blest all you who weep,
for the Kingdom of God is there in your eyes.
    Alas for you who do your laughing now,
    you who make pleasure the object of your life;
    alas for you who don't know how to weep!

How blest you who are pure,
and whose heart is sincere as the heart of a child.
How blest you who are pure,
you who sacrifice all in a self-gift of love.
How blest you who are pure,
for the Kingdom of God is there in your heart.
    Alas for you who imagine you are pure,
    who keep your body and your mind shut on yourself;
    alas for you who don't know how to give!

How blest you who are poor,
amen I say you will never see death.


MARIE-CLAIR PICHOUD
TRS. H. J. RICHARDS

Then Jesus took his disciples up the mountain,
and gathering them around him he taught them saying:

Blessed are the poor in spirit for theirs is the kingdom of heaven.
Blessed are the meek.
Blessed are they that mourn.
Blessed are the merciful.
Blessed are they who thirst for justice.
Blessed are all the concerned.
Blessed are you when persecuted.
Blessed are you when you suffer.
Be glad and rejoice for your reward is great in heaven.
Try to remember what I'm telling you.

Then Simon Peter said,
    Will this count?
And Andrew said,
    Will we have a test on it?
And James said,
    When do we have to know it for?
And Philip said,
    How many words?
And Bartholomew said,
    Will I have to stand up in front of the others?
And John said,
    The other disciples didn't have to learn this.
And Matthew said,
    How many marks do we get for it?
And Judas said,
    What is it worth?
And the other disciples likewise.

Then one of the Pharisees who was present
asked to see Jesus' lesson plan
and inquired of Jesus
his terminal objectives in the cognitive domain.

And Jesus wept.


DON LINEHAN

Blessed are those who are too tired, busy or disorganised
    to meet with their fellow Christians on Sunday each week –
    they are my best workers.
Blessed are those who enjoy noticing the mannerisms
    of clergy, choir and servers –
    I can see their heart is not in it.
Blessed are the Christians who wait to be asked
    and expect to be thanked –
    I can use them.
Blessed are the touchy –
    with a bit of luck they can even stop going to church.
Blessed are those who keep themselves
    and their time and their money to themselves –
    they are my missionaries.
Blessed are those who claim to love their God
    at the same time as hating other people –
    they are mine forever.
Blessed are the troublemakers –
    they shall be called my children.
Blessed are those who have no time to pray –
    they are easy prey to me.
Blessed are you when you read this
    and think it is about other people and not about yourself –
I've got you.


THE DEVIL'S BEATITUDES
ANON

# 2  POVERTY

## *Scripture Readings*

Why does God not set a Judgment Day?
Why do his faithful never see justice?

The wicked come and move boundary marks,
evicting the shepherd and his whole flock;
they rob the orphan of his ass,
and seize the widow's cow in pawn,
her fatherless child snatched from her breast:
the children of the poor become payments for debt.
Beggars now are thrust off the road,
and all the poor must be hidden from sight.
They wander like wild asses searching for food
from dawn to dusk, but their children starve.

They bring in the harvest for wicked landlords,
and strip the vineyards of grapes for the rich,
but they have no clothes to cover their backs,
and they starve to death as they bring their sheaves;
they press the rich man's oil from the olives,
they tread his winepress, and yet go thirsty.
All night they lie, with nothing to cover them,
unprotected from the cold,
drenched by rainstorms from the hills,
clinging to the rocks for shelter.

From out of the city come the groans of the dying,
and the gasp of the wounded crying for help:
but God is deaf to their appeal.


JOB 24:1-12

The galaxies sing the glory of God
    and Arcturus 20 times larger than the sun
and Antares 487 times more brilliant than the sun
Dorado Sigma with a brightness of 300,000 suns
and Orion Alpha which is equal
    to 27,000,000 suns
Aldebaran with its diameter of 32 million miles
    Lyra Alpha 300,000 light years away
and the nebula of Boyer
    200 million light years away
all announce the work of your hands . . .

The sun describes a gigantic orbit
around the constellation Sagittarius
– he is like a bridegroom who leaves his wedding bed
and travels surrounded by his planets at 45,000 miles per hour
towards the constellation of Hercules and Lyra
(and takes 150 million years to make his circle)
and does not deviate an inch from his orbit

The Law of the Lord stills the subconscious
    it is as perfect as the law of gravity
its words are like the parabola of comets
its decrees like the centrifugal spin of galaxies
its precepts are the precepts of the stars
that eternally remain fixed in their positions
    and their speeds
    and their respective distances
and cross one another's route a thousand times
    and never collide
The judgments of the Lord are just
    and not like propaganda
and worth more than dollars
    and stocks and bonds

Keep me from the arrogance of money and political power
and I will be free of all crime
    and major offence
and may the words of my poems be pleasing to you
Lord my Liberator


PSALM 19 (18)
TRS. ERNESTO CARDENAL (B. 1915)

15

# God of the Poor

My father told me about God.
He said, The city where we live
is a city without peace.
But there will come a city
filled with peace
and it will cover the whole world . . .

There shall be no more rich and poor,
no kings, no slaves,
no more hunger, no more aggression,
but light enough and bread for everyone.
That is God's dream, what God wills.

I shivered from happiness,
and each time I heard these words
it was the same.
My father said,
That city people build by doing good.
God is the still small voice within
that speaks to you
and tells you what is good
in a voice that you can understand,
so that you also know how to do right
for the one who is beside you.

Not because blind fate
rules this universe,
not because the world is poor
and nature vicious,
but because the strongest rule,
and the strong kill the weak,
and those with money and power
desire still more –
that is why the world topples.

You who live in this godforgotten world,
do not forget who you are yourself:
a drop of water, a seed on the wind,
flowers in the open field,
sharer of all.

But also remember his name – 'God of the poor' –
and remember the son of man
who was the spokesman for that God,
and seek a place where people
speak and live in his spirit.
And learn to understand that voice
that speaks to you from far off and within
to tell you what is good.
So that you choose to stand on the side of the poor,
and to walk down their road.


Huub Oosterhuis




## *Like a Pauper*


Thou (God) shalt not refuse to answer
    anyone who cries to thee with all his heart.
Thou shalt not despise the poor wretch
    who implores thee for mercy.
Thou shalt not turn thy creature away from thy door
    empty-handed.
Thou shalt not grieve him or shame him over his sin.
Thou shalt not remember against him
    his past sins, hidden in his heart.
Thou shalt not banish him who strays,
    but shalt draw near him.
Thou shalt not turn away from any complaint
    when I stand before thee like a pauper.


10th century Hebrew Acrostic

# *Poorest of the Poor*

In Brazil I sat with a woman – a mother – on a bare hillside. She and her people have lost almost all of their land. Nothing would grow on this woman's hillside. There was one dirty stream at the bottom of the hill with a few fish. Otherwise there was nothing to eat. Two yards in front of where we sat was a small circle of wooden crosses. It was where she buried her children beneath the dust. She had had no food or medicine to keep them alive.

The parable of the sheep and the goats ('the least of my brethren') suggests that God is like that woman; that when I think of God, I should think of turning and praying to someone like her. What shall I offer such a God when I come to worship? And what shall I expect such a God to do for me when I am frightened and in trouble? And when I pray, what shall I say to such a God – this woman who has nothing at all?

I sat beside her as part of a world that crucifies her and shuts her out – that refuses to stretch out its hand to feed her and clothe her and visit her, or comfort her children. Yet, like the crucified, her arms are open wide in welcome. She greets me as a friend. She offers to share what she has, and she thanks me for coming.

That is the Advent God who came in Jesus of Nazareth. That is Emmanuel, God with us, forever empty and forever full – who comes and comes again in the poorest of the poor.

MICHAEL TAYLOR

# Poverty and Emptiness

My field is desolate, unsown,
my maiden body quiet as a tomb.
No seed of life will now be blown
by breath of man into my womb.

But should this dry and fallow field
by some much greater Breath be blown upon,
quickened and hallowed, it will yield
fruits that will last when yours are gone.

I know that God will richly bless
this hitherto unlovely thing and wild.
My poverty, my emptiness,
await God's gift, a virgin's Child.


P. DE ROSA (B. 1932)


# Brother to the Poor

That man in Rome
is our brother in Jesus Christ.
He is a brother to the poor of Haiti . . .
I wish him well in his life,
and in his sacred mission.
I honour him and love him
as I love all my fellow men and women.
Trouble is,
he does not love me in return.


JEAN BERTRAND ARISTIDE

# Learning from the Poor

When Somoza ruled Nicaragua, he attended Mass every Sunday. I do not believe in that God. (*Daniel Ortega 1985*)

If the concept of God has any validity or any use, it can only be to make us larger, freer and more loving. If God cannot do this, then it is time we got rid of him. (*James Baldwin 1963*)

The poor accept God: they hear the Gospel not so much as truth, but as good news ... What they do humanizes us, it evangelizes us. (*Jon Sobrino 1991*)

The theology of liberation is one of the great gifts of the poor of Latin America to Christianity, as well as to the middle class of the rich world, to which I belong. It is a gift which is not used up; it nourishes me, as it nourishes the poor ...

The most important thing I have learned from the poor is what I recognize in the losing battles we are involved in here in the west ... We fight against every new war toy which our masters consider necessary and profitable, but the militarization not only of our country but also of our brains continues to advance ... In all these struggles, the greatest danger for us lies in becoming tired and giving up, letting ourselves be diverted or corrupted, falling into dependence on drugs, alcohol or prosperity, becoming depoliticized because we submit ourselves to the idol of oppression, who whispers to us with a soft voice: 'Nothing can be done about it'.

From the poor of Latin America I learn their hope, their toughness, their anger, and their patience. I learn a better theology in which God is not Lord-over-us but Strength-in-us; in which the miracles of Jesus are not distinguished from ours – we too drive out demons and heal the sick. I learn to trust in the people of God ... I begin to hunger and thirst after righteousness. I am evangelized.

DOROTHEE SOELLE

# *Woe to the Rich*

Not even you
with your irresistible look
of infinite goodness
succeeded in moving
the heart
of the rich young man.
And yet he, from his childhood
had kept
all the commandments.
Lord, my Lord, may we never
out of mistaken charity
water down
the terrible truths
you have spoken to the rich.


DOM HELDER CAMARA

# 3  LOWLINESS

## *Scripture Readings*

You're not to worry about what you're going to eat,
or about what you're going to wear;
what you are more important than anything you eat,
more important than what you wear.

Look at the wild birds, they don't go out farming,
they don't go building barns like farmers do;
it is God who must see that they get enough to eat:
don't you trust him to look after you?

Look at the flowers, the flowers growing wild,
they don't work at home like mothers have to do;
it is God who fits them out looking better than a king:
don't you trust him to look after you?

Look at the long grass blowing in the wind:
it is God who chose its texture and its hue;
yet tomorrow it will be just a bonfire on the farm:
don't you trust him to look after you?


THE GOSPEL OF MATTHEW 6:25-30

My soul, now glorify
the Lord who is my Saviour;
rejoice, for who am I
that God has shown me favour?

The world shall call me blest
and ponder on my story:
in me is manifest
God's greatness, and his glory.

For those who are his friends
and keep his laws as holy,
his mercy never ends,
and he exalts the lowly.

But by his power the great,
the proud, the self-conceited,
the kings who sit in state,
are humbled and defeated

He feeds the starving poor,
he guards his holy nation,
fulfilling what he swore
long since in revelation.

Then glorify with me
the Lord who is my Saviour:
one holy Trinity
for ever and for ever.


THE GOSPEL OF LUKE 1:46-55
ANON

Tell out, my soul, the greatness of the Lord!
Unnumbered blessings, give my spirit voice;
tender to me the promise of his word;
in God my Saviour shall my heart rejoice.

Tell out, my soul, the greatness of his name!
Make known his might, the deeds his arm has done;
his mercy sure, from age to age the same;
his holy name – the Lord, the Mighty One.

Tell out, my soul, the greatness of his might!
Powers and dominions lay their glory by;
proud hearts and stubborn wills are put to flight,
the hungry fed, the humble lifted high.

Tell out, my soul, the glories of his word!
Firm is his promise, and his mercy sure.
Tell out, my soul, the greatness of the Lord
to children's children and for evermore!


THE GOSPEL OF LUKE 1:46-55
TRS. TIMOTHY DUDLEY-SMITH (B. 1926)

# *Fragilely*

What heart could have thought you?
Past our devisal
(O filigree petal!)
Fashioned so purely,
Fragilely, surely,
From what Paradisal
Imagineless metal,
Too costly for cost?
Who hammered you, wrought you,
From argentine vapour?

'God was my shaper.
Passing surmisal,
He hammered, he wrought me,
From curled silver vapour,
To lust of his mind –
Thou couldst not have thought me!
So purely, so palely,
Tinily, surely,
Mightily, frailly,
Insculped and embossed,
With his hammer of wind,
And his graver of frost.'

FRANCIS THOMPSON (1859-1907)

# Amazing grace

Exceedingly odd
Is the means by which God
Has provided our path to the heavenly shore:
Of the girls from whose line
The true light was to shine
There was one an adulteress, one was a whore.
There was Tamar, who bore –
What we all should deplore –
A fine pair of twins to her father-in-law;
And Rahab the harlot,
Her sins were as scarlet,
As red as the thread which she hung from the door;
Yet alone of her nation
She came to salvation,
And lived to be mother of Boaz of yore;
And he married Ruth,
A Gentile uncouth,
In a manner quite counter to biblical lore;
And of her there did spring
Blessed David the King
Who walked on his palace one evening, and saw
The wife of Uriah,
From whom he did sire
A baby that died, oh, and princes a score.
And a mother unmarried
It was too that carried
God's son, and him laid in a cradle of straw,
That the moral might wait
At the heavenly gate
While the sinners and publicans go in before,
Who have *not* earned their place
But received it by grace,
And have found them a righteousness not of the Law.

MICHAEL D. GOULDER

# Take Away our Pride

O God of earth and altar,
bow down and hear our cry:
our earthly rulers falter,
our people drift and die;
the walls of gold entomb us,
the swords of scorn divide;
take not thy thunder from us,
but take away our pride.

From all that terror teaches,
from lies of tongue and pen,
from all the easy speeches
that comfort cruel men,
from sale and profanation
of honour and the sword,
from sleep and from damnation
deliver us, good Lord!

Tie in a living tether
the prince and priest and thrall,
bind all our lives together,
smite us and save us all;
in ire and exultation,
aflame with faith and free,
lift up a living nation,
a single sword to thee.


G. K. Chesterton (1874-1936)

# *Dumb*

When fishes flew and forests walked
    And figs grew upon thorn,
Some moment when the moon was blood
    Then surely I was born.

With monstrous head and sickening cry
    And ears like errant wings,
The devil's walking parody
    Of all four-footed things.

The tattered outlaw of the earth
    Of ancient crooked will;
Starve, scourge, deride me, I am dumb,
    I keep my secret still.

Fools! For I also had my hour,
    One far fierce hour and sweet:
There was a shout about my ears,
    And palms before my feet.


G. K. CHESTERTON (1874-1936)

# Before an Icon

The unbeliever is challenged
The intellectual is lost for words
The theologian feels small
The artist's heart is filled with joy
The contemplative finds fresh inspiration
Those who are distressed find peace
Those who thought they were strong are disarmed
The wounded find healing
The fainthearted find confidence
The thirsty are refreshed
The poor man listens and understands
The child throws wide its arms, and smiles.


ANON

# Gentle and Low

God bless the grass that grows through the crack,
they roll the concrete over it to try and keep it back;
the concrete gets tired of what it has to do,
it breaks and it buckles and the grass grows through,
and God bless the grass.

God bless the truth that fights toward the sun,
they roll the lies over it and think that it is done;
it moves through the ground and reaches for the air,
and after a while it is growing everywhere,
and God bless the grass.

God bless the grass that breaks through cement,
it's green and it's tender and it's easily bent,
but after a while it lifts up its head,
for the grass it is living and the stone it is dead,
and God bless the grass.

God bless the grass that's gentle and low,
its roots they are deep and its will is to grow;
and God bless the truth, the friend of the poor,
and the wild grass growing at the poor man's door,
and God bless the grass.

MALVINA REYNOLDS

# 4 BROKEN HEARTS

## *Scripture Readings*

When God pulls down what he built up,
and roots up what he planted,
then friends of his must take their luck:
no special treatment's granted.

When God sends ruin on the land,
the outcome there's no saying;
you must take your life in hand
and search for strength in praying.

THE PROPHET JEREMIAH 45:4-5

The Lord is quick to heed the poor
and liberate them from their chains.
The Lord is close to broken hearts:
he rescues slaves, and sets them free.

PSALM 34(33):17-18

# Being Hurt

The Skin Horse had lived longer in the nursery than any of the others. He was so old that his brown coat was bald in patches and showed the seams underneath, and most of the hairs in his tail had been pulled out to string bead necklaces . . .

'What is real?' asked the Rabbit one day, when they were lying side by side near the nursery fender, before Nana came to tidy the room. 'Does it mean having things that buzz inside you and stick-out handles?'

'Real isn't how you are made', said the Skin Horse. 'It's a thing that happens to you. When a child loves you for a long time, not just to play with, but really loves you, then you become real.'

'Does it hurt?' asked the Rabbit.

'Sometimes,' said the Skin Horse, for he was always truthful. 'But when you are real you don't mind being hurt.'

'Does it happen all at once, like being wound up,' he asked, 'or bit by bit'

'It doesn't happen all at once,' said the Skin Horse. 'You become. It takes a long time. That's why it doesn't often happen to people who break easily, or who have sharp edges, or who have to be kept carefully. Generally, by the time you are real, most of your hair has been loved off, and your eyes drop out and you get loose in the joints and very shabby. But these things don't matter at all, except to people who don't understand.'

MARGERY WILLIAMS

# The Cost of Pain

Nothing can make up for the absence
of someone whom we love,
and it would be wrong to try and find a substitute;
we must simply hold out and see it through.
That sounds very hard at first,
but at the same time it is a great consolation,
for the gap, as long as it remains unfilled,
preserves the bonds between us.
It is nonsense to say that God fills the gap;
he does not fill it, but on the contrary, he keeps it empty
and so helps us to keep alive our former communion with each other,
even at the cost of pain.

DIETRICH BONHOEFFER (1906-1945)

# In Our Sorrow

Everlasting God,
help us to realise more and more
that time and space are not the measure of all things.
Though our eyes do not see,
teach us to understand
that the souls of our dear ones are not cut off.
Love does not die,
and truth is stronger than the grave.
Just as our affection and the memory of the good they did
unite us with them at this time,
so may our trust in you lift us
to the vision of the life that knows no death.

God of our strength,
in our weakness help us;
in our sorrow comfort us;
in our confusion guide us.
Without you our lives are nothing;
with you there is fullness of life for evermore.

JEWISH FUNERAL PRAYER

# *A Bleeding Heart*

'Abraham! Abraham! –
  'Lord, thy will be done' –
'Go and take now, Abraham,
  Thy son, thy only son;
And offer him with wood and fire
A sacrifice on Mount Moriah'.

'Father, father Abraham . . . '
  'Here am I, my son' –
'Behold the wood and fire; but lamb
  For offering see I none.'
'My child,' a bleeding heart replied,
'The lamb will God himself provide.'

'Abraham! Abraham!' –
  'Angel, here I stand' –
'Yonder thicket hides a ram;
  Stay thy faithful hand:
And God will bless and multiply
The sons whom thou didst not deny.'

Praise the God of Abraham,
  Who sacrificed his own,
His blessed Son, to be the Lamb
  That sits upon the throne;
Whose heart bled on till it was done,
And did not spare his only Son.


MICHAEL D GOULDER

## Returning the Jewels

The two young sons of Rabbi Meir both died on the same day. It happened on a Sabbath afternoon, while he was still at the synagogue for the service.

When he came home, his wife Beruria refused to break the sad news to him straight away: it would ruin the joy that he always took in the Sabbath. She waited till the evening. Finally she plucked up courage. 'Can I ask you a question?' she said.

'Of course.'

'Some time ago, a friend gave me some jewels to look after for him. He came today and asked to have them back. What shall I do?'

The Rabbi was puzzled. 'What a strange question. I'm surprised at you asking it. You've obviously got to return the jewels.' She then led him to the room where the children lay dead, and said, 'These are the jewels I have to return.'

Rabbi Meir broke down. All he could do was to sob out the words of Job:

'The Lord has given, and the Lord has taken away; blessed be the name of the Lord.'

THE TALMUD (5TH CENTURY)


## This Diminishment

When a Christian suffers he says,
'God has touched me' – which is true,
but only at the *end* of a series of spiritual stages.
For when a Christian suffers he should *begin* by saying,
'God wants to free me from this diminishment;
God wants me to help him to take this cup from me.'
To combat an ill that threatens us
is unquestionably the first act of our Father in heaven;
it would be impossible to conceive of him in any other way,
and still more impossible to love him.
It is a perfectly correct view of things –
and strictly consonant with the Gospel –
to regard Providence across the ages
as brooding over the world
in a ceaseless effort to spare it its wounds
and bind up its hurts.

PIERRE TEILHARD DE CHARDIN (1881-1955)

# *Against All Tribulations*

This word, 'Thou shalt not be overcome'
was said full sharply and full mightily
for sickness and comfort
against all tribulations that may come.
He said not, 'Thou shalt not be troubled',
'Thou shalt not be travelled (burdened)',
'Thou shalt not be dis-eased (distressed)';
but he said, 'Thou shalt not be overcome.'
God will that we take heed at this word,
and that we be ever mighty
in faithful trusting in weal and woe;
for he loveth us and liketh us:
and so will he that we love him and like him,
and mightily trust in him,
and all shall be well.


JULIAN OF NORWICH (1342-1416)

# About Suffering

When the ram's horn sounds, and three stars appear (or ought to) in the sky, the Jewish Day of Atonement begins, and I recite a lot of prayers. Most I go along with, but one or two bits I leave out and hope no one notices. It's no good telling God what he knows I can't say sincerely.

I have always had trouble with this sentence:

Thou O God art just in all that has come upon us, for Thou hast done justly, but we have acted wickedly.

For me it's over the top. A lot of suffering in my life is my own fault, but at my last Judgment God has also got some explaining to do . . .

You can't cure suffering, but you aren't helpless either. Don't despise small things . . . holy objects, prayer books, rosaries and religious medals help in pain. They're something solid to clutch on to. Get your suffering outside you. Turn it into a letter or short story, or draw it on a piece of paper. If you're not up to creative stuff, complain to a friend . . .

Don't get snobbish about your suffering. It isn't a punishment for your sins, nor a reward for your virtue. It's part of being human – that's the name of the game . . . Because you're human, allow yourself to scream or moan, or buy a salt beef sandwich, or a second opinion. God prefers humility to heroics.

And talking of God . . . if you offer your suffering to God, it seems to turn it inside out and gives your pain some meaning. Though what it means I'm not sure. Are you?

'It's a hard life being human', my grandpa said. But it's interesting and you don't die of boredom.

LIONEL BLUE (B. 1930)

# 5 HUNGER FOR JUSTICE

## Scripture Reading

I sing of God's coming in judgment,
God's verdict on justice gone wrong:
'How long will you bear with injustice,
and put up with humbug – how long?

'Your task was to rescue the needy,
to give their rights to the poor,
to defend the defenceless in prison,
and throw wide open their door.

'But no! You've all lost your senses,
your finer feelings are dead;
you wander about in your darkness,
you have stood the world on its head!

'I had thought you could speak for me,
enthroned like gods at my right.
I was wrong: you're mortal like others,
and you'll fall from a very great height!'

O God, you must come and pass judgment,
you alone can bring justice to birth,
you alone, the Ruler of nations,
you alone, the Judge of the earth.


PSALM 82 (81)

## Feeding The Hungry

In the future world, people will be asked,
'What was your occupation?'
If they reply, 'I fed the hungry',
then they will be told, 'This is the gate of the Lord;
those who feed the hungry, let them enter.' (Psalm 118:20.)
It is the same with giving drink to the thirsty,
clothing the naked, looking after orphans,
and generally any deed of loving kindness.
All these are gates of the Lord,
and those who do such deeds shall enter within.

JEWISH MIDRASH ON THE PSALMS.

## I Was Hungry

I was hungry and you blamed it on the Communists
I was hungry and you circled the moon
I was hungry and you told me to wait
I was hungry and you set up a commission
I was hungry and you said, 'So were my ancestors'
I was hungry and you said, 'We don't hire over 35's'
I was hungry and you said, 'God helps those . . .'
I was hungry and you told me I shouldn't be
I was hungry and you told me machines do that work now
I was hungry and you had defence bills to pay
I was hungry and you said, 'The poor are always with us'
Lord, when did we see you hungry?

ANON

# *Sharing*

Let's share the food, my brother,
Let's share the fruits of the earth,
Steak for me and rice for you,
Eggs for tea and rice for you,
It's nice for me, but rice for you;
Fruit and wine and milk and jam,
Cheese and pickles and fish and ham
For me;
    And a little rice, just a little rice
    (If you're lucky) for you.

Let's share the pain, my brother,
You shall have more than your share.
Pains for you and pills for me,
Germs for you and jabs for me,
Though you die young, long life for me;
Tranquillisers, deep X-ray,
Penicillin, and nothing to pay,
For me;
    And a little clinic, just a mobile clinic
    (Per hundred thousand people) for you.

Let's share the world, my brother,
Apartheid means equal shares.
Your land for us, and mine for me,
Sand for you, and soil for me,
What's left for you, the best for me;
Schools and bridges, roads and trains,
Oil and tractors, libraries, 'planes,
For me;
    And a nice reserve, yes, a nice reserve
    (When your working life is over) for you.

Let's share the war, my brother,
Let's share the horrors of war.
Peace for me, napalm for you,
Trade for me, but raids for you,
Away for me, at home for you,
Cripples, orphans, refugees,
Villages burned, no leaves on trees,
For you;
    And a little pang of conscience, just a little twinge
    (Not very often) for me.

Let's share our wealth, my brother,
Let's share all that you have.
Gold for me, and beads for you,
Christ for me, the devil take you,
There's two for me, and none for you;
Bingo, bombs, and drugs, and booze,
Money to burn and waste and lose
For me;
    And a little aid, just a little Christian aid
    (When we can spare it), for you.


JIM STRINGFELLOW

## To Make Men Free

Mine eyes have seen the glory of the coming of the Lord:
he is trampling out the vintage where the grapes of wrath are stored;
he hath loosed the fateful lightning of his terrible swift sword:
his truth is marching on.

He hath sounded forth the trumpet that shall never call retreat;
he is sifting out the hearts of men before his judgment seat;
O be swift, my soul, to answer him; be jubilant, my feet!
Our God is marching on.

In the beauty of the lilies Christ was born across the sea,
with a glory in his bosom that transfigures you and me;
as he died to make men holy, let us live to make men free,
while God is marching on.


JULIA WARD HOWE (1819-1910)


## Fighting For Justice

Jesus wasn't a priest.
He was a poor man fighting for justice,
spending his life with people,
and healing the sick.
That is the theology of liberation.
We're simply putting it into practice.


JEAN BERTRAND ARISTIDE

# Speaking Out

First they came for the Jews,
and I didn't speak out
because I wasn't a Jew.
Then they came for the Communists,
and I didn't speak out
because I wasn't a Communist.
Then they came for the Trade Unionists,
and I didn't speak out
because I wasn't a Trade Unionist.
Then they came for the Catholics,
and I didn't speak out
because I was a Protestant.
Then they came for me,
but by that time,
there was no one left to speak out.

PASTOR MARTIN NIEMOELLER (1892-1984)

# Making Trouble

Christian society in Britain has domesticated the Gospel.
It is geared to loving God in moderation.
We may give alms to the poor,
visit the sick and the lonely,
hold annual bazaars and flag days for those in need –
in fact do any good works
which do not threaten the pattern of our society.
But to question the way in which public money is spent on housing,
or to request admission of foreign refugees to our country,
becomes at once a 'political' act.
When we demand justice
at the expense of other people's comfort or security
we become 'troublemakers'.

SHEILA CASSIDY (B.1937)

# To Demand Justice

Give us, O Lord, churches
that will be more courageous than cautious;
that will not merely comfort the afflicted,
    but afflict the comfortable;
that will not only love the world,
    but will also judge the world;
that will not only pursue peace,
    but also demand justice;
that will not remain silent
    when people are calling for a voice;
that will not pass by on the other side
    when wounded humanity is waiting to be healed;
that will not only call us to worship,
    but also send us out to witness;
and that will follow Christ
    even when the way points to a cross.

To this end we offer ourselves
in the name of him who loved us
and gave himself for us. Amen.

CHRISTIAN CONFERENCE OF ASIA 1982

# *Wading In*

While I believe violence is evil, I am convinced that there are situations in which it is to be encouraged. I no longer accept the view long proclaimed by the Church that in life we are always faced by a choice between good and evil. In the real world, the choice is often between two or more evils, and the challenge is to select the lesser or least of the alternative evils . . .

Take for example the Good Samaritan. What would he have done if his donkey had run faster and he had arrived on the scene earlier? Would he have reined in his animal and waited on the other side of the road until the robbers had finished beating the poor man and taken off with their spoils? Or should he have waded into the fight and tried to beat the robbers off with his whip? Has a Christian not the right, even the duty, to use counter-violence against unjust violence? . . .

And suppose that the Good Samaritan passed the same way every week, and nearly every time he found someone who had been beaten up and robbed. Would he fulfil his Christian duty simply by binding up the wounds of each and taking them to hospital at his expense? Rather, would he not have to recognize that he was dealing, not with casual violence, but with institutionalized violence, and – while helping the victims – concentrate his major effort on finding and eliminating the source?

GARY MACEOIN

There are three distinct kinds of violence, not only one. The media have made us very familiar with the violence of protests, strikes, and in extreme cases armed struggle. But these are almost all cases of what may be called Violence II. Violence II is simply a response to Violence I, where the situation itself is violent, because it has become institutionalized in systems and structures.

It is not easy to recognise Violence I. If we are born into it and grow up within it, it becomes so much part of the scenery that we can remain unaware of it. But if it deprives people of their rights, if it oppresses and exploits and dehumanises them, then it is bound to blow up into the revolt that is Violence II. Which itself inevitably leads to the repression that is Violence III.

> Violence is the only way of ensuring a hearing for moderation. (*William O'Brien, Irish Nationalist, 1905*)
>
> It is those who make the peaceful revolution impossible, who make the violent revolution inevitable. (*President J. F. Kennedy*)
>
> A riot is the expression of a people who have not been listened to. (*Martin Luther King, assassinated 1968.*)

Christians of the past have too easily said, 'We should accept all our crosses as the will of God.' But surely what God wills is the liberation of people. Surely what God wants is for people to be freed from injustice, exploitation and oppression, from unemployment, hunger and disease, from all systems in which basic human rights are denied them. And if these systems have become so fossilised that no amount of discussion can change them, then it is the will of God that they be destroyed.

And if people have become so much part of the system that they do not even notice how unjust it is ('The walls of gold entomb us', wrote G. K. Chesterton), then they too may have to have violence done to them if they are to be liberated. Few people in the northern hemisphere are aware that by keeping for ourselves what others basically need, we practice a form of violence against these others. Few people anywhere in the world are aware that when we see others only in terms of the advantage they can be to us, we do violence to them.

Here is a handful of quotations which might throw a little more light on the matter:

> The Christian who is not a revolutionary is living in serious sin. (*Camillo Torres*)
>
> To all intents and purposes, it is today illegal to be an authentic Christian. Why? Because the world around us is founded on an established disorder. To proclaim the Gospel against this disorder is subversive. (*Archbishop Oscar Romero, 1917-1980*)
>
> There is no way to peace along the road of security. Peace must be dared. It is the great venture. It can never be made safe. Peace is the opposite of security. (*Dietrich Bonhoeffer, 1934*)

Take the resistance fighters of occupied Europe, who used violence against their Nazi oppressors in World War II. We do not call them 'terrorists'? Why? Because we accept that their cause was just and their methods disciplined. If Christians refuse to condemn the use of violence in the attempt to end injustice, it is because they recognize that we have no right to condemn the use of violence by others in pursuit of justice, if we are prepared to use it ourselves for the same end.

H. J. RICHARDS (B. 1921)


# No Reconciling Good and Evil

Much theology today takes 'reconciliation' as the key to the resolving of problems. On the face of it this may sound very Christian. But is it? The fallacy here is that 'reconciliation' has been made into an absolute principle that must be applied in all cases of conflict or dissension.

But not all cases of conflict are the same. We can imagine a private quarrel between two people or two groups whose differences are based upon misunderstandings. In such cases it would be appropriate to talk and negotiate in order to sort out the misunderstandings and to reconcile the two sides.

But there are other conflicts in which one side is right and the other wrong. There are conflicts where one side is a fully armed and violent oppressor while the other side is defenceless and oppressed. There are conflicts that can only be described as the struggle between justice and injustice, good and evil, God and the devil. To speak of reconciling these two is not only a mistaken application of the Christian idea of reconciliation, it is a total betrayal of all that Christian faith has ever meant.

Nowhere in the Bible or in Christian tradition has it ever been suggested that we ought to try to reconcile good and evil, God and the devil. We are supposed to do away with evil, injustice, oppression and sin – not come to terms with it.

THE KAIROS DOCUMENT 1985

# 6  TENDERNESS

## *Scripture Reading*

Praise God who forgives all our sins,
and heals us of everything evil,
who rescues our life from the grave,
and clothes us in mercy and love.

Our God is all kindness and love,
so patient and so rich in pity,
not treating us as we deserve,
not paying us back for our sins.

As heaven is high above earth,
so strong is his love for his people;
as far as the east from the west,
so far he removes all our sins.

As fathers take pity on sons,
so God will show us his compassion,
for he knows of what we are made:
he knows we are no more than dust.

PSALM 103 (102) 1-14

## In the Palm of Your Hand

Because of our many sins,
where shall we hide, O Lord?
In the heavens?
There resides your majesty and your glory!
In the bottom of the earth?
There your hand is all-powerful!
Even in the caves of the earth
your presence is all-pervading.
We rather come to you, O merciful Lord,
and hide in the palm of your hand,
for your love is immeasurable
and your tenderness without limit.

HYMN FROM THE OCTO-ECHOS CYCLE IN THE BYZANTINE LITURGY

## A Forgiving God

To commit a sin against a fellow human being is worse than committing
a sin against God. The person you harm may move to a different
address, and you may never have the opportunity of asking for
forgiveness. But God is everywhere, and you can always get his
forgiveness when you look for him.

SAYINGS OF THE HASIDIM (18TH CENTURY)

# The Gentle Path

Throw away your rod,
throw away your wrath;
O my God,
take the gentle path!

For my heart's desire
unto yours is bent:
I aspire
to a full consent.

Then let wrath remove;
love will do the deed:
for with love
stony hearts will bleed.

Throw away your rod;
though men frailties have,
you are God:
throw away your wrath!

GEORGE HERBERT (1593-1633)

# Like God

The holy hermit Makarios came home one day to find a desert thief in his hut. He stood by like an obliging stranger, and helped the thief to load his animal, and finally led him out, holding his finger to his lips.

Makarios, the brethren said, was like God, who shields the world and bears its sins; so did he shield his brothers, and when one of them sinned, he would neither hear nor see.

HELEN WADDELL (1889-1965)

# *Whoever Does Not Love*

Basically, there are two kinds of law:
    law as the way things ought to be,
    for example, No Trespassing,
    and law as the way things are,
    for example, the law of gravity.
God's law has traditionally been spelled out
    as a law of the first kind,
    a compendium of do's and don'ts;
But do's and don'ts are in fact the work of moralists,
    to keep us from each other's throats.

God's law is the work of God
    and comes under the second category,
    a statement of the way things are.
It is summed up in eight words in 1 John 3:14:
    'Whoever does not love remains in death.'

Like it or not, that's how it is.
If you don't believe it, you can always test it,
    as you can test the law of gravity
    by walking out of a tenth storey window.


F. BUECHNER

## *Put Hatred To Sleep* *(Genesis 21-22)*

Ishmael, my brother,
how long shall we fight each other?

My brother from times bygone,
my brother – Hagar's son,
my brother, the wandering one.

One angel was sent to us both,
one angel watched over our growth –
there in the wilderness, death threatening through thirst,
I a sacrifice on the altar, Sarah's first.

Ishmael, my brother, hear my plea:
it was the angel who tied thee to me . . .

Time is running out, put hatred to sleep.
shoulder to shoulder, let's water our sheep.


SHIN SHALOM (B.1904)

# Poisonous Hatred

I was angry with my friend: I told my wrath, my wrath did end.
I was angry with my foe: I told it not, my wrath did grow.
And I watered it in fears, night and morning with my tears,
And I sunned it with my smiles, and with soft deceitful wiles,
And it grew both day and night, till it bore an apple bright,
And my foe beheld it shine, and he knew that it was mine,
And into my garden stole, when the night had veiled the pole,
And took the fruit, and ate it, whole;
In the morning glad I see my foe outstretched beneath the tree.


WILLIAM BLAKE (1757-1827)

# Love or Law?

The Christian ethic can never honestly be presented as law plus love, or law qualified by love, *however much safer that would be*. There is no question that law has its place, but that place is at the boundaries, and not at the centre. This was the revolution which Jesus represented for the Pharisees. His teaching was not a reform of legalism but its death . . .

A faithful Jew stayed as close as possible to the observance of the law even when he had to depart from it. Jesus stayed as close as possible to the fulfilment of human need, no matter how wide of the law this led him.

And this, of course, as the Scribes well saw, is terribly dangerous doctrine. It needs its checks and balances: it cries aloud for letters to the church press . . . and exhortations to return to 'the Law of God' as the foundation of moral life.

But this is what the New Testament refuses to allow us to do . . . The ten commandments are not the basis of Christian morals, on which an ethic of love goes on to build. Of course the commandment of love does not contradict or relieve men of the obligations of the old; it summarizes them and immeasurably deepens them.

In fact in the Sermon on the Mount Jesus takes several of them, pointing through them and beyond to the unconditional claim of God upon man and of person upon person they were framed to safeguard. But in the process he destroys them *as law* . . .

The deeper one's concerns for persons, the more effectively one wants to see love buttressed by law. But if law usurps the place of love because it is safer, that safety is the safety of death . . .

The Sermon on the Mount does not say in advance, 'This is what in every circumstance or in any circumstance you must do', but, 'This is the kind of things which at any moment, if you are open to the absolute unconditional will of God, the Kingdom, or love, can demand of you.' It is 'relevant' not because it solves our moral problems (that is the kind of relevance we are always asking for), but because it transforms us (and that is the kind of relevance we don't ask for, but which in the end is what changes us and the world). In other words, Jesus' purpose was not to order the fruit, but to make the tree good (Matthew 12:33).

JOHN A. T. ROBINSON (1919-1983)

# A Close Thing

Two farmers, Ibrahim and Yussef, needed to go to Damascus for supplies. Yussef was anxious about leaving his sick mother for such a long time, so Ibrahim offered to take Yussef's camel along with his own camel, and do the shopping for both of them.

Before Ibrahim set off with the two camels, Yussef anxiously demanded an assurance that his own camel would be well looked after; it wasn't used to being away from his master for days on end. Ibrahim assured Yussef he would treat his camel exactly like his own.

The days passed. Again and again Yussef would walk up to the brow of the hill to see if Ibrahim was on his way back. Then eventually he saw the three figures, a man leading two camels. But as they came closer, he noticed that one of the camels was looking far more weary and dejected than the other. To his horror, he realised it was his own camel.

'What's gone wrong?' he worriedly asked Ibrahim, when he eventually arrived. 'Why is your camel so much sprightlier than mine?'

'I have no idea', replied Ibrahim.

'Did you feed him?'

'Of course, he had exactly the same food as my camel.'

'Did you water him?'

'Of course, he drank exactly the same amount as my camel.'

'Did you rest him?'

'Of course, every night they both lay down together, and I lay down between them. But I have to confess that as we all went to sleep, I put my head closer to my camel than to yours.'

AN ARAB STORY

# *Vague Good Will*

One can always find warm hearts
who, in a glow of emotion,
would like to make the whole world happy,
but who have never attempted the sober experiment
of bringing a real blessing to a single human being.
It is easy to revel enthusiastically
in one's love of man,
but it is more difficult to do good to someone
solely because he is a human being.
When we are approached by a human being
demanding his right,
we cannot replace definite ethical action
by mere vague good will.
How often has the mere love of one's neighbour
been able to compromise and hold its peace!


LEO BAECK (1873-1956)


# *People*

I love the human race.
It's people I can't stand.


ANON.

# No Longer Enemies

In '41 Mama took us back to Moscow. There I saw our enemies for the first time. If my memory is right, nearly twenty thousand German war prisoners were to be marched in a single column through the streets of Moscow.

The pavements swarmed with onlookers, cordoned off by soldiers and police. The crowd were mostly women – Russian women with hands roughened by hard work, lips untouched by lipstick and thin hunched shoulders which had borne half the burden of the war. Every one of them must have had a father, a brother or a son killed by the Germans.

They gazed with hatred in the direction from which the column was to appear.

At last we saw it. The generals marched at the head, massive chins stuck out, lips folded disdainfully, their whole demeanour meant to show superiority over their plebeian victors. 'They smell of eau-de-cologne, the bastards,' someone in the crowd said with hatred. The women were clenching their fists. The soldiers and policemen had all they could do to hold them back.

All at once something happened to them. They saw German soldiers, thin, unshaven, wearing dirty, bloodstained bandages, hobbling on crutches or leaning on the shoulders of their comrades; the soldiers walked with their heads down.

The street became dead silent – the only sound was the shuffling of boots and the thumping of crutches.

Then I saw an elderly woman in broken-down boots push herself forward and touch a policeman's shoulder, saying, 'Let me through.' There must have been something about her that made him step aside.

She went up to the column, took from inside her coat something wrapped in a coloured handkerchief and unfolded it. It was a crust of black bread. She pushed it awkwardly into the pocket of a soldier, so exhausted that he was tottering on his feet. And now suddenly from every side women were running towards the soldiers, pushing into their hands bread, cigarettes, whatever they had.

The soldiers were no longer enemies. They were people.

YEVGENY YEVTUSHENKO (B.1933)

# Levity of Love

No revolution will come in time
    to alter this man's life
    except the one
    surprise of being loved.
He has no interest in Civil Rights,
    neo-Marxism,
    psychiatry,
    or any kind of sex.
He has only twelve more hours to live,
    so never mind about
    a cure for cancer, smoking, leprosy
    or osteo-arthritis.
Over this dead loss to society
    you pour your precious ointment,
    call the bluff
    and laugh at the
Fat and clock-faced gravity
    of our economy.
    You wash the feet
    that will not walk tomorrow.
Come, levity of love,
    show him, show me,
    in this
    last step of time,
Eternity,
    leaping and capering.

SYDNEY CARTER (B.1925)

# Brotherly Love

Before anyone ever thought of building a town there, Jerusalem was a cornfield owned and worked by two brothers, one of whom was single, and the other married, with several children.

One autumn, when they had harvested the ripe grain, and stacked it in two equal heaps as agreed between them, the single brother got up at night saying, 'My brother has a wife and children to support, and needs more corn than I do.' So he quietly moved some of his sheaves to his brother's pile.

The married brother also woke up saying, 'My brother is all alone, without the comfort of wife and children, and needs more corn than I do.' So he quietly moved some of his sheaves to his brother's pile.

So the two stacks remained equal, and it is on that spot that the Temple now stands.

ARAB LEGEND

# 7  SINCERITY

## *Scripture Reading*

If your hand should corrupt you, amputate!
Handicap is a better fate
than having two hands full of hell:
    O the worm undying, terrifying
    fire you cannot quell.

If your foot should corrupt you, chop it off!
Better to limp, though people scoff,
than to stride surefooted to hell:
    O the worm undying, terrifying
    fire you cannot quell.

If your eye should corrupt you, out with it!
Short sight's a greater benefit
than a clear-eyed vision of hell:
    O the worm undying, terrifying
    fire you cannot quell.


THE GOSPEL OF MARK 9:43-48

# *In Tune With God*

Non vox sed votum,
Non clamor sed amor,
Non cordula sed cor
Psallit in aure Dei.
Lingua consonet menti,
Et mens concordet Deo.

It is not the voice but the choice,
Not the clarity but the charity,
Not the harp but the heart
That makes music in the ear of God.
Let your tongue reflect your thoughts,
And your thoughts be in tune with God.

16TH CENTURY INSCRIPTION IN THE CHURCH OF SAN DAMIANO, ASSISI.
TRS. H. J. RICHARDS (B.1921)

# *Witness to Truth*

May my life be one link in a chain of goodness.
As I say the prayers of my fathers,
help me to remember their devotion and faithfulness,
their joy and suffering, which are in every word.
Holiness is my heritage: may I be worthy of it.

May this tradition live in me, and pass from me
to generations I shall never know,
enriched by the truth that I have found
and the good deeds I have done.
So may I fulfill my task on earth, and receive my blessing.

And when the service ends and the prayers have ceased,
help me to bring their spirit into the world in which I live.
May I love God above all,
and my neighbour as myself,
and be a living witness to the truth that never changes. Amen.


JEWISH SABBATH MORNING SERVICE

# Priorities

The other day a Zambian dropped dead not a hundred yards from my front door. The pathologist said he'd died of hunger. In his shrunken stomach were a few leaves and what appeared to be a ball of grass. And nothing else.

That same day saw the arrival of my *Methodist Recorder*, an issue whose columns were electric with indignation, consternation, fever and fret at the postponement of the final report of the Anglican-Methodist Unity Commission . . . It took an ugly little man with a shrunken belly, whose total possessions, according to the police, were a pair of shorts, a ragged shirt and an empty Biro pen, to show me that this whole Union affair is the great Non-Event of recent British Church history . . .

So I have undergone something of a conversion on the question of Anglican-Methodist Union. Not from pro. to con. or vice versa. But to a sort of functional neutrality in that I don't give a damn which way the vote goes as long as we get the whole business out of the way and regain our sanity. Either side can buy my vote for a quid's donation to Oxfam . . .

I don't really care whether I end up in a Union Church or as a residual Methodist. I don't really care whether I am ordained, re-ordained, reconciled or commissioned by bishops, presidents, priests or presbyters. I don't care *where* they put the words of Absolution, so long as there is some point in the Service at which I can unload my conscience, over-burdened with the knowledge of what we have done to that little man with the shrunken belly in the name of Christ.

Lenny Bruce cut to the heart of the matter in a single biting epigram. He said, 'I know in my heart, by pure logic, that any man who claims to be a leader of the Church is a hustler if he has two suits in a world in which most people have none' . . . The real obscenity, which should stick in our throats and choke us, is what we have done in Christ's name to degrade that little man with a shrunken stomach with all our pious concern and carefully doled out charity and fervent prayer and passionate assurances that we intend to get around to his plight when we have put our own house in order.

Colin Morris

# *Commitment*

Lord, make me a means of your peace.
Where there is hatred caused by fear and intolerance,
   let me sow love, in your gentleness.
Where there is vengefulness caused by injustice,
   let me sow forgiveness, which brings reconciliation.
Where there are doubts about the power of love
     over weapons in resolving conflicts,
   let me sow the faith that comes with knowing that you,
   who are mightier than all things, are love itself.
Where there is despair of being able to do anything
     to turn human hearts away from war,
   let me sow the hope that comes
   with realization that we are not alone,
   for you are working with us and through us.
Where there is the darkness caused by the shadow of war,
   let me sow the light of your wisdom
   that illuminates for us the way of peace.
And where there is sadness caused by death
   in violence and conflicts,
   let me sow the joy of your promise
   of new and eternal life.

Father, we can do these things
   if you help us to realize
   that it is in giving them to others
   that we, in turn, receive them too,
   that it is in pardoning others
   who harm or upset us
   that we are pardoned by you.
And that it is in giving our whole lives to you,
   to be spent bringing your message of love and peace
   for all people, and not just our friends –
   in short, dying to ourselves,
   that we are given eternal life in your kingdom.


PRAYER OF ST FRANCIS
EXPANDED BY PAX CHRISTI USA

# Clear Sight

I set a riddle to the rulers of the land:
Is your God's Law dearer than a man's right hand?
Would you be sons of God or sons of man?
And don't you hear the children, for they understand?
    Let's play a game:
    let's pretend their ox has fallen lame,
    let's see if God's Law remains the same.

I set a riddle as I hung on a tree,
as I stretched out my arms across eternity,
as I drew the whole world in from the ends of the sea,
and I gave it to the children who were following me.
    Let's play a game:
    let's pretend that love is each man's name,
    let's see if the world remains the same.

Here's a riddle of the fire, that is the strength of the weak,
the wealth of the poor and the power of the meek,
that the blind can see, of which the dumb can speak,
and a fire only found in the children who will seek.
    Let's play a game:
    you're the ring of roses, I'm the flame,
    just to bring this fire was why I came.


MALCOLM STEWART

# God's Diary, 10 January 510 BC

A genius has appeared in India, full of My Spirit.
He illustrates perfectly
the fact that My word has always been heard
by all the nations of the earth,
and My light enlightened
everyone coming into My world.
But there are few who have become
as enlightened as My son Siddhartha Gautama.
I'm particularly intrigued by the fact
that his approach to Me is so different
from the Jewish approach
that he seems at times to be saying the very opposite.
But he knows, as few do,
that in religious matters in particular,
there are many truths, not one.
To insist that I'm not to be thought of as an object,
whether of knowledge or of love,
he has taken to calling Me 'The Void, The Emptiness'.
I like this.

I liked it still more
when his disciples recently expressed concern
that what he taught
was not to be found in the Holy Books.
'Then put it in,' he said.
'But some of the things you say
contradict what the Books say.'
'Then change the Books.'
I could do with more people of such insight.
And with such a sense of the sacred.
And with such compassion for My world.


H. J. RICHARDS (B. 1921)

# 8  PEACEMAKING

## *Scripture Reading*

How welcome on the mountains are the feet of those
who bring the news of peace,
who bring the gospel of salvation to Jerusalem:
'Our God reigns!'

The watchmen raise their voices in a shout of joy
as they see the Lord;
they see the Lord returning to Jerusalem:
Our God reigns!

Break into song, you ruins of Jerusalem,
the Lord has brought us peace;
the ends of all the earth have seen his saving power:
Our God reigns!


THE BOOK OF ISAIAH 52:7-10

# In the Same Embrace

I came to the Holy Land to give, and behold I was overwhelmed by what I received. I came to enrich and purify, and behold I was the one to be enriched and purified.

I loved the family of the Lord. His family are both the Jews and the Arabs. I held the Muslim, the Druze, the Jew, the Christian, everyone, believer and unbeliever, in the same embrace. How I yearned to hold them to my heart and show them all how they can live together, love together, and see the radiance of God in each other's face.

Was that not the vision of Christ in the Gospel? The divine beauty in each race needed only the opportunity to mingle, embrace and dance together, and the more we did this, the more permanent the situation became. Christ was not wrong: 'If you love as I have loved' the world will be a heaven.

The Holy Land of Israel will, some day, be that heaven.

Cultures, all cultures, Jewish and Christian and Muslim, are of God. People, all people, are holy, sacred and good. But people, all people, of all cultures and all religions, always need 'conversion'. Conversion is openness, understanding, respect, even awe in the presence of each other, and forgiveness. This is the conversion preached by the Gospel.

So I tried to identify with Jews and Arabs. It is possible! Anyone who opens his heart to them can see in each other's face the face of God. They have the warmth of a mother's womb. If only we could create a little more understanding. Understanding wipes out suspicion. Love will flower and bloom.

ARCHBISHOP JOSEPH RAYA

# The Uniforms They Wear

The humble, the gentle, the merciful, the just,
the devout and loyal souls all belong to one religion;
and when death takes away the masks,
they will recognise each other,
even though the different uniforms they wear here
makes them look like strangers.


WILLIAM PENN (1644-1718)


# The Difference

For Methodists,
    what is allowed is allowed,
    and what is not allowed is not allowed.
For Anglicans,
    what is allowed is allowed,
    and what is not allowed is also allowed.
For Roman Catholics,
    what is not allowed is not allowed,
    and what is allowed is also not allowed.


ANON

# *Being Nice*

The Christians are so nice,
so awfully nice;
they are the nicest people in the world.

And what's more, they're very nice about being nice,
about your being nice as well!
If you're *not* nice they soon make you feel it.

Buddhists and Muslims and Jews and so on,
they're all very well,
but they're not *really* nice, you know.
They're not nice in *our* sense of the word, are they now?

That's why one doesn't have to take them seriously.
We must be nice to them, of course,
of course, naturally –
But it doesn't really matter what you say to them,
they don't really understand.
Just be nice, you know! Oh, *fairly* nice,
not *too* nice of course, they take advantage;
but nice enough, just nice enough
to let them feel they're not *quite* as nice as they might be.


ADAPTED FROM D. H. LAWRENCE (1885-1930)

# *What Song Do You Sing?*

There is one who sings the song of his own soul,
and in his soul he finds everything,
full spiritual satisfaction.

And there is one who sings the song of the people.
For he does not find the circle of his private soul
wide enough, and so goes beyond it,
reaching for more powerful heights.
And he unites himself with the soul of the community,
sings its songs, suffers with its sorrows,
and rejoices in its hopes . . .

And there is one whose soul lifts beyond
the limitations of his community,
to sing the song of mankind.
His spirit expands to include
the glory of the human image and its dreams . . .

And there is one who lifts beyond this level,
until he becomes one with all creation
and all creatures and all the worlds.
And with all of them he sings a song . . .

And this is the song of holiness,
the song of God.


RABBI KOOK, CHIEF RABBI OF PALESTINE (1865-1935)

# The Non-Believer

Jesus was once taken to a football match. At the first goal he cheered wildly and threw his hat in the air. When the other side equalised, he again went wild with delight. A man behind him asked, 'Which side are you on?'

'Neither', he replied, 'I'm just enjoying the game.'

'What are you?' the man asked. 'An atheist or something?'

ANON

# Fundamentally Decent Men

Somewhere in a university town in the United States there lives a brilliant research chemist . . . I would make an inspired guess that he is a decent, kindly man, because most people are. It was his technical virtuosity which made possible the addition of an extra ingredient to napalm so that the burning jelly would stick with greater tenacity to human skin, defying the efforts of its victim or doctors to scrape it off until it had done its disfiguring work.

No doubt, every morning before that brilliant man set off for his laboratory, he would fondly kiss the skin of his children without making any conscious mental connection between that simple fatherly act and the complex chemistry in which he was totally absorbed – otherwise he would have gone stark, staring mad. It makes no sense whatever to call that man sinful, except to the extent we are all sinful. It may be true that at some point he must accept moral responsibility for the uses to which his research is put. Yet the ultimate infamy which produces wards full of children roasting alive in war-zones issues from an infinite series of decisions taken by fundamentally decent men, any one of whom would cut off his arm rather than do direct violence to a child.

COLIN MORRIS

# Five Ways to Kill a Man

There are many cumbersome ways to kill a man:
You can make him carry a plank of wood
to the top of a hill and nail him to it. To do this
properly you require a crowd of people
wearing sandals, a cock that crows, a cloak
to dissect, a sponge, some vinegar and one
man to hammer the nails home.

Or you can take a length of steel,
shaped and chased in a traditional way,
and attempt to pierce the metal cage he wears.
But for this you need white horses,
English trees, men with bows and arrows,
at least two flags, a prince and a
castle to hold your banquet in.

Dispensing with nobility, you may, if the wind
allows, blow gas at him. But then you need
a mile of mud sliced through with ditches,
not to mention black boots, bomb craters,
more mud, a plague of rats, a dozen songs
and some round hats made of steel.

In an age of aeroplanes, you may fly
miles above your victim and dispose of him
by pressing one small switch. All you then
require is an ocean to separate you, two
systems of government, a nation's scientists,
several factories, a psychopath and
land that no one needs for several years.

These are, as I began, cumbersome ways
to kill a man. Simpler, direct, and much more neat
is to see that he is living somewhere in the middle
of the twentieth century, and leave him there.


EDWIN BROCK

# Helpless Tears

Just a little rain falling all around,
the grass lifts its head to the heavenly sound,
just a little rain, just a little rain,
what have they done to the rain?

Just a little boy standing in the rain,
the gentle rain that falls for years.
And the grass is gone, the boy disappears,
and rain keeps falling like helpless tears,
and what have they done to the rain?

Just a little breeze out of the sky,
the leaves pat their hands as the breeze blows by,
just a little breeze with some smoke in its eye,
what have they done to the rain?


MALVINA REYNOLDS

# 9  PERSECUTION

## *Scripture Readings*

Cursed be the morn,
the morn when I was born,
soft stranger to the earth;
no benediction
on the day of that affliction
called my birth.

Cursed be the man,
the man who quickly ran
to my father, and thus cried:
'Your wife's had a boy,
my tale is of nothing but joy',
for he lied.

No joy did I bring,
that wrinkled nurseling thing,
my wretched father's son;
cursed be the mite
who should have brought only delight:
he brought none.

Great God, tell me why,
tell me why I did not die
when they severed my birth cord?
Why make me survive,
in my sorrows more dead than alive?
Tell me, Lord.

Then my God replied:
'Jeremiah, if you had died,
my own word would have died too.
My word is your child:
to mother it, gentle or wild,
I chose you.'

THE PROPHET JEREMIAH 20:14-18 AND 1:9
TRS. P. DE ROSA (B.1932)

My God my God why have you abandoned me?
I am only a mockery of a man
    a disgrace to the people
They ridicule me in all their newspapers

Armoured tanks surround me
I am at machine gun point
    encircled by barbed wire
All day long they call my name from the rolls
They tattooed a number on me
They have photographed me among the barbed wire
all of my bones have been counted as in an X-ray
They have stripped me of all identity
They have brought me to the gas chamber
and divided among them my clothes and my shoes

I cry out begging for morphine and no one hears me
I cry out in the straitjacket
I cry out all night in the asylum of mad men
in the ward of terminal patients
in the quarantine of the contagiously sick
in the halls of the old people's home
Isquirm in my own sweat in the psychiatric clinic
I suffocate in the oxygen tent
I weep in the police station
in the army stockade
    in the torture chamber
    in the orphanage
I am contaminated with radioactivity
    and fearing infection no one comes near me

Yet I will speak of you to my brothers
I will praise you in the meetings of our people
My hymns will resound in the midst of this great people
The poor will sit down to a banquet
Our people will celebrate a great feast
This new generation soon to be born


PSALM 22 (21)
TRS. ERNESTO CARDENAL (B. 1915)

# Stand Fast

But if you live the time
that no man will give you good counsel,
nor no man will give you good example;
when you shall see virtue punished
and vice rewarded;
if you will then stand fast
and firmly stick to God,
upon pain of my life,
though you be but half good,
God will allow you for whole good.

St Thomas More (1478-1535)

# I Might Have Been The Persecutor

O Lord, I beseech you,
make me thankful for the grace you have given me.
As for those who persecute me,
in the name of religion,
thinking they are doing your will,
pardon them, in your mercy.
For if you had revealed to them
what you have revealed to me,
they would not be acting as they are.
And if you had hidden from me
what you have hidden from them,
I might have been the persecutor instead of the persecuted.
Glory to you in all you do.
Glory to you in all you will.

Prayer of Al-Hallaj al-Mansur

# God's Suffering People

I saw under the altar the souls of those who had been slain for the word of God and for the witness they had borne; they cried out with a loud voice, 'O Sovereign Lord, holy and true, how long wilt thou judge and avenge our blood on those who dwell on the earth?' Then they were each given a white robe and told to rest a little longer, until the number of their fellow servants and their brethren should be complete, who were to be killed as they themselves had been.
*(Revelation 6:9-11)*

It is for judgment that God's suffering people pray when they cry, 'How long, Lord?' Most commentaries condemn this prayer thunderously and immediately. This is not Christian, they say; it is a nullification of the teaching of Jesus . . . People who do not know what oppression and suffering is react strangely to the language of the Bible. The truth is that God *is* the God of the poor and the oppressed. Although they do not count for much in the eyes of the powerful and the rich, their blood *is* precious in God's sight. Because they are powerless, God will take up their cause and redeem them from oppression and violence. The oppressed do not see any dichotomy between God's love and God's justice . . . God takes up the cause of the poor and the oppressed precisely because in this world their voices are not heard – not even by those who call themselves Christians. God even has to take up the cause of the poor *against* 'Christians'. Christians who enjoy the fruits of injustice without a murmur, who remain silent as the defenceless are slaughtered, dare not become indignant when the suffering people of God echo the prayer of the psalms and pray for deliverance and judgment. In the midst of indescribable pain and appalling indifference, this prayer – and the certainty of God's loving response – has become our sustenance. Even as the dictators of this world rise up to issue a new threat, we know: 'The Lord reigns.' *How* God does it is for God to decide. That God *shall* do it is our faith and joy.

ALLAN BOESAK (B.1945)

# For My Fellow Jews

When I visit great cathedrals,
graven images delight and frighten me,
tourist of holy sites as many
of my generation, inhabited by
a people I no longer live with.
But always I am glad that there,
in these lofty, not always friendly places,
David, Isaiah, thin-lipped Jeremiah
and the first Joseph appear,
in painted stone or many-coloured glass,
their strong Judaic faces
modelled by compatriots perhaps, or
gentiles who looked the part, royal,
prophetic, wise and singularly
unusurious. Art, though not wholly adequate,
consoles an inherited grief, and somewhere
amongst the alien guttering candles
and incenseful entreaties
a kaddish[1] becomes possible.

Perfervid in panes of molten glass
Jews, smitten with light, burn
most graciously, or swathed
in corn-gold stone hold an oblique dignity.
Stone wrought by craftsmen at their height
does not melt away, like candle-wax,
or cakes of holocaustic soap
this century crafted also in Europe.

When I visit great cathedrals
I am baffled by stacked candles
which do not smell like a menorah[2]
and the inexplicable priest who has failed
to put on skull cap and tallith[3]
to maintain his stand there.

NADINE BRUMMER

1 *kaddish*    – prayer for the dead
2 *menorah*    – seven-branched candelabrum used at feast of lights and
                symbolically, to represent Jewish struggle.
3. *tallith*    – prayer-shawl

## Do Unto Others

As soon as I had said it I was sorry. By using the German word I had tried to humiliate him. My desire to humiliate this young man was causing me to feel guilty, and yet at the same time I asked myself why I should feel hurt for wanting to hurt the German.

Then it occurred to me that this was the argument of the SS: to hurt, to kill the Jew is not a sin; it is an act of delousing. The feelings I was experiencing were not my own feelings, but theirs. I felt confused. I was doing to him what they had done to me. I was persecuting an innocent man whose only sin was that he happened to be born in Germany.

EUGENE HEIMLER (B.1922)

## Umbrian Frescoes

The walls appeal – those conical breasts
offered to Christ – bambini,
and angels swinging with great cheerfulness.

They corner most scenes. Naive wings
worn formally as extra limbs,
make you believe in them as facts

you wish could happen now; until that Pietà
and that small angel witnessing, who acts
quite humanly, lifts both hands to his head,

warding off an agonizing sound.
You almost hear the long drawn-out Christ,
and feel his white pelt weighing down

the woman's accurate lap. You realise
the helplessness of angels, and that your own
full-grown frightened hands are fluttering

like nervous wings. Should they go or stay?
Brings cups of tea or wipe the sweat away?
Or turn the volume down?

NADINE BRUMMER

# 10  BIDDING PRAYERS

That oppressed people and those who oppress them
    may free each other;
That those who are handicapped and those who think they are not
    may help each other;
That those who need someone to listen
    may touch the hearts of those who are too busy;
That the homeless may bring joy
    to those who open their doors reluctantly;
That the lonely may heal those
    who think they are self-sufficient;
That the poor may melt the hearts of the rich;
That seekers for truth may give life
    to those who are satisfied they have found it;
That the dying who do not want to die
    may be comforted by those who find it hard to live;
That the unloved may be allowed to unlock
    the hearts of those who cannot love;
That prisoners may find true freedom
    and liberate others from fear;
That those who sleep in the streets may share their gentleness
    with those who cannot understand them;
That the hungry may tear the veil from the eyes of those
    who do not hunger after justice;
That those who live without hope may cleanse the hearts
    of their brothers and sisters who are afraid to live.
That the weak may confound the strong, and save them;
That violence may be overtaken by compassion;
That violence may be absorbed by men and women of peace;
That we may all be healed;

Give us the grace, good Lord
to labour for these things that we pray for.


THÉRÈSE VANIER

# 11   A SELECTION OF COLLECTS

1

Lord God,
we see the sins of the world
in the light of your only Son.
Since his coming
to be your mercy toward us,
we have come to see
how hard and unrelenting
we are toward each other.
We ask you to renew us
and remake us in his image.
Let us grow like him
and no longer repay evil with evil,
but make peace and live in truth
today and every day of our lives.

2

God, we witness
unheard of things.
You, God, have given power
to Jesus of Nazareth
to be merciful to others
and to forgive them.
We ask you, God,
for this power, this freedom
to be a healing grace
to all those who live with us
in this world,
as a sign that you are
the forgiveness of all sins.

3

Lord God,
your kingdom is here
hidden and close to us –
someone to care for
and people to live for.
Your will is done on earth
everywhere where people
live and die for each other.
We pray therefore
that we may gradually
accomplish this from day to day,
and thus come to know your name,
and find you,
our Father for ever.

4

Why, God, are we divided,
why are we broken?
Can you not cure and save us
as you saved our brother Jesus
from the power of death?
We call upon you in his name:
make us whole again
and restore us in honour;
renew the shape of this world
against every sin,
and cover us with your light,
your Holy Spirit.

5

God, you are merciful to us
in all our doings, good and bad.
You do not insist on your right
but acquit us
and accept us.
Everything is possible with you.
Give us the spirit to follow you,
make us merciful to each other
so that the world may know
who you are:
nothing but love, our Father,
God.

6

Lord God,
your constant love of humanity
has been handed down to us
in human words.
In this way you are our God and Father.
We pray that we may eagerly listen
to the words of your gospel,
and in this way be with you heart and soul
in the fellowship of the Holy Spirit.

7

Lord our God, we thank you
for you are a God of people,
for we may call you our God and our Father,
for you hold our future in your hands,
for this world touches your heart.
You called us and broke through our deafness,
you appeared in our darkness,
you opened our eyes with your light,
you ordered everything for the best for us
and brought us to life.
Blessed are you, the source of all that exists.
We thirst for you,
because you have made us thirsty.
Our hearts are restless
until we are secure in you
with Jesus Christ, our Lord.
With all who have gone before us in faith,
we praise your name, O Lord our God.
You are our hope
and we thank you, full of joy.

8

God our Father,
we have sinned against you
in thought, word and deed:
we have not loved you with all our heart;
we have not loved our neighbour as ourselves.
But you have kept faith with us.
Have mercy on us;
strip us of all that is un-Christian,
and help us live up to our calling,
through Jesus Christ, our Lord.

9     Mighty God,
we lift up our hearts to you
in gratitude for your love to us.
Take our lives –
our work and our leisure,
the ordinary things of life and the special things,
the sadness and joy we know and have known.
Accept, we pray, our praise and thanksgiving
as we offer our very selves to you
in worship and adoration,
through Jesus Christ, our Lord.

10     Let us remember God, everlastingly great,
utterly loving, wholly to be trusted.
And because God knows us through and through,
because God loves us better than we love ourselves,
because we need not pretend to him, and cannot,
let us quietly acknowledge our need
of his forgiveness and renewal.
God, have mercy on me,
sinner that I am.

*11*    We pray for reconciliation between religions.
May those who profess one faith
no longer suspect and misrepresent
those who profess another.
May good be recognized wherever it exists.
May all people hold to truth as they see it,
and bear witness to it,
but with goodwill and respect.
And may the Christ who came to reconcile
Jew and Gentile, slave and freeman into one body,
continue to break down the walls which divide us.

*12*    You have created us to live in peace
but still man lifts his hand against his brother.
We try to make amends, but our efforts
to establish peace by force do not work out.
As nations we need you to forgive us, O God,
and to teach us new ways of peace.
O God, let each man be his brother's keeper
through Jesus Christ, our Lord.

13

Heavenly Father,
on our own we know that we are weak and timid:
but your promises, coming to us from Christ,
give us strength and courage.
He has named the devil, put him in his place,
and exposed the final weakness of evil.
He has said, 'Yes, there is truth;
there is grace; there is goodness.'
He has made us see where we stand,
and what we must do,
and we are surprised at the quiet strength within,
which gives us the courage that does not fail.
We give you thanks,
through Jesus Christ, our Lord.

14

Send your Spirit,
God, here among us,
friendship and truth,
life overflowing.
Make us free
from anxiety and bitterness,
free for everyone
who is our neighbour,
so that our hands
may build up peace –
houses of peace
for our children.
Hasten the time
when your future is established,
the new creation
where you are our light,
all in all.

**15**

O God,
send us your Spirit
who is life, justice and light.
You want the well-being of all people,
not their unhappiness
and not death.
Take all violence away from us.
Curb the passion
that makes us seek each others' lives.
Give us peace on earth
by the power of Jesus Christ,
your Son among us.
We ask and implore you
to grant this.

# Index of Authors and Translators

# Acknowledgements

Except where mentioned, the scripture readings in this anthology are translations by H. J. Richards, © copyright 1995 by Kevin Mayhew Ltd.

The publishers wish to express their gratitude to the following for permission to reproduce copyright material in this publication:

Nadine Brummer for *For My Fellow Jews* and *Umbrian Frescoes*. (New Blackfriars, Nov. 1993)

Catholic Herald Ltd, Herald House, Lambs Passage, Bunhill Row, London EC1Y 8TQ for *Making Trouble*, an extract from the Sheila Cassidy interview from the 'Catholic Herald' dated 1 October 1977.

Geoffrey Chapman Publishers, Wellington House, 125 Strand, London WC2R 0BB for *Blest are you* by James Quinn SJ, *You are blessed* by Malcolm Stewart and *How blest you who are poor* by Marie-Clair Pichoud, trs. H. J. Richards.

Christian Aid, PO Box 100, London SE1 7RT for *Poorest of the Poor*, which is taken from a Christmas leaflet © Christian Aid 1989.

Christian Conference of Asia, Pak Tin Village, Mei Tin Road, Shatin, N. T., Hong King for *To Demand Justice* © 1982 Christian Conference of Asia.

Columba Press, 93 The Rise, Mount Merrion, Blackrock, Co Dublin, Eire for *God's Diary 19 January 510 BC*, which is taken from 'God's Diary' by H. J. Richards © 1991 Columba Press.

Constable & Co Ltd, 3 The Lanchesters, 162 Fulham Palace Road, London W6 9ER for *Like God*, from 'The Desert Fathers' by Helen Waddell.

The Council of Churches for Britain and Ireland, Inter-Church House, 35-41 Lower Marsh, London SE1 7RL for *No Reconciling Good and Evil*, from 'The Kairos Document' © The Kairos Theologians 1985. Originally published in the UK by BCC/CIIR.

Peter De Rosa for *Poverty and Emptiness* and *Cursed be the morn*.

Bishop Timothy Dudley-Smith, 9 Ashlands, Ford, Salisbury, Wiltshire SP4 6DY for the hymn text *Tell out, my soul*.

Edition du Seuil, 27 Rue Jacob, 75261 Paris, France for *This Diminishment*, taken from 'Le Milieu Divin' by Pierre Teilhard de Chardin, trs. Barbara Wall.

Epworth Press, Hartley Victoria College, Luther King House, Brighton Grove, Manchester M14 5JP for *Priorities*, from 'Include Me Out' by Colin Morris, Epworth Press 1968, and *Fundamentally Decent Men,* from 'The Hammer of the Lord' by Colin Morris, Epworth Press 1973.

*Continued overleaf*

Professor Michael Goulder for *Amazing Grace* and *A Bleeding Heart*, both © Michael Goulder.

HarperCollins Publishers Ltd, 77-85 Fulham Palace Road, Hammersmith, London W6 8JB for *Whoever Does Not Love*, from 'Wishful Thinking, A Theological ABC' by F. Buechner, Colllins 1973.

Harvill Press, 84 Thornhill Road, London, N1 7RD for *No Longer Enemies* from 'A Precocious Autobiography' by Yevgeny Yevtushenko, first published in the English language by E. P. Dutton and Co, New York. First published in Great Britain by Collins Harvill 1967. © in the English translation E. P. Dutton & Co. Inc. Reproduced by permission of the Harvill Press.

Hodder Headline plc, 338 Euston Road, London NW1 3BH for *About Suffering*, from 'Blue Horizons' by Lionel Blue © 1989 Hodder & Stoughton.

McCrimmon Publishing Co Ltd, 1-12 High Street, Great Wakering, Southend-on-Sea, Essex SS3 0EQ for *How lucky you are*, from 'The Beatitudes for Children' by H. J. Richards © 1988 McCrimmon Publishing Co Ltd.

Mowbrays, an imprint of Cassell plc, Wellington House, 125 Strand, London, WC2R 0BB, for *Learning from the Poor*, from 'Celebrating Resistance' by Dorothee Soelle, Mowbray 1993.

Orbis Books, PO Box 308, Maryknoll, New York, 10545-0308, USA for *Brother to the Poor*, from 'In the Parish of the Poor: Writings from Haiti' by Jean Bertrand Aristide © 1990 Orbis Books.

Pantheon Books, 201 East 50th Street, New York, NY 10022, USA for *Vague Good Will*, from 'The essence of Judaism' by Leo Baeck. Reprinted by kind permission of Schocken Books, published by Pantheon Books, a division of Random House, Inc.

Reform Synagogues of Great Britain, The Sternberg Centre for Judaism, 80 East End Road, Finchley, London N3 2SY for *Feeding the Hungry* and *Do Unto Others*, from 'Returning – Exercises in Repentance' edited by Rabbi Dr. Jonathan Magonet and *Put Hatred to Sleep*, *Witness to Truth*, *What Song do you Sing?* and *In Our Sorrow*, from 'Forms of Prayer for Jewish Worship' © Reform Synagogues of Great Britain, London 1977.

SCM Press Ltd, 9-17 St Albans Place, London N1 0NX for *The Cost of Pain*, from 'Letters and Papers from Prison, The Enlarged Edition' by Dietrich Bonhoeffer © SCM Press 1971; *Love or Law?* , from 'Christian Freedom in a Permissive Society' by J. A. T. Robinson, SCM Press 1970; the Collects numbered 7, 9 and 10 from 'Contemporary Prayers for Public Worship' ed. Caryl Micklem, SCM Press 1967, and the collects numbered 8, 11, 12 and 13 from 'More Contemporary Prayers' ed. Caryl Micklem, SCM Press 1970.

Search Press Ltd, Wellwood, North Farm Road, Tunbridge Wells, Kent, TN2 3DR, for *The Galaxies Sing* and *Psalm 22*, from 'Psalms of Struggle and